ID0887405

POEMS OF THE BLACK OBJECT

FUTUREPOEM BOOKS
NEW YORK CITY
2015

POEMS OF THE BLACK OBJECT

Ronaldo V. Wilson

Second printing © 2015 by Ronaldo Wilson
First published in paperback by Futurepoem books in 2009
ISBN: 978-0-9822798-0-9

This edition first published in paperback by Futurepoem books
P.O. Box 7687 JAF Station, NY, NY 10116
www.futurepoem.com
Executive Editor: Dan Machlin
Managing Editor: Jennifer Tamayo
Guest Editors: Tan Lin, Frances Richard, Jerome Sala

Cover design: Mickel Design (http://www.mickeldesign.com) and HR Hegnauer
Stingray image on exterior and interior cover: S. G. Goodrich Animal Kingdom
    Illustrated Vol 2 (New York: Derby & Jackson, 1859)

Typesetting & copyediting: *typeslowly* design (cjmattison@gmail.com) and HR Hegnauer
Typefaces: NotCaslon by Mark Andresen, 1991 (Cover); Eldorado (Text)
Printed in the United States of America on acid-free paper

NYSCA

This project is supported in part by the New York State Council on the Arts with the support of Governor Andrew Cuomo and the New York State Legislature, as well as by our Kickstarter backers, individual donors and subscribers. Futurepoem books is the publishing program of Futurepoem, Inc., a New York state-based 501(c)3 non-profit organization dedicated to creating a greater public awareness and appreciation of innovative literature.

Distributed to the trade by Small Press Distribution, Berkeley, California
Toll-free number (U.S. only): 800.869.7553
Bay area/International: 510.524.1668
orders@spdbooks.org
www.spdbooks.org

Acknowledgments:

Acknowledgments to the following journals where these poems, some in earlier versions, are published: "The Black Object's Catalyst," "The Black Object's Deportment," *The Encyclopedia Project, Vol. 1. A-E;* "The Black Object's Memory," "The Black Object's Elasticity," *nocturnes (re)view of the literary arts;* "The Breaker's Pose," "The Breaker's Performance," *Callaloo;* "Brutal End," *Provincetown Arts;* "Chronophotographe," *FENCE* and *Shankpainter;* "Construction of a Black Poetic Self in Four Narratives," *FENCE;* "Dream in a Fair," *The Encyclopedia Project, Vol. 2. F-K;* "Illicit Traffic," *Interim;* "In-An-Imprint,"(excerpt) *Black Renaissance Noire,* and in *Urban Dialect* as part of *Quotes Community: Notes for Black Poets* ed. Thomas Sayers Ellis; "The Lesson," *New York City Law Review;* "On the C Train the Black Object Ponders Amuzati's Family Eaten in the Congo," *Callaloo;* "Self Portrait as Excess O, O Self Selves," *Cave Canem IV;* "Vergelioian Space V: Caliban X" and "Vergelioian Space VI: Open Letter to Faith Ringgold and Michele Wallace," *nocturnes (re)view of the literary arts.*

The author wishes to thank those writers who have offered invaluable guidance and support, at various stages, through this project: Dawn Lundy Martin, Duriel E. Harris, Meena Alexander, David Rivard, Joshua Weiner, Jennifer Jazz, Yusef Komunyakaa, Michele Wallace, Wayne Koestenbaum, Erica Hunt, Claudia Keelan, giovanni singleton, John Keene, Mendi Lewis Obadike, Tisa Bryant, and R. Erica Doyle. Much gratitude to everyone at Futurepoem books: Frances Richard, Tan Lin, Jerome Sala, and Dan Machlin for selecting this volume, as well as for offering their keen and thoughtful comments, and thanks to Jeremy Mickel and Christopher Mattison for their wonderful book design, outside and in.

Notes:

The book's opening quotes are from Frantz Fanon's *Black Skin, White Masks* (New York: Grove Press, 1967) and Toi Derricotte's *The Black Notebooks: An Interior Journey* (New York: Norton, 1999). The quote from John Stainton in "Dream In A Fair" is taken from a wikinews.org article on Steve Irwin's death dated 9/4/2006. The quote from Shakespeare's Caliban in "The Breaker's Pose," as well as the quotes from Ariel in "Vergelioian Space IV: The Bulimia Method" and "Ariel's Freeze" are from Shakespeare's *The Tempest,* edited and introduced by Stephen Orgel (Oxford: Oxford University Press, 1994). The poems in the section *Vergelioian Space* are part of a group of poetic interruptions with which the author flooded the Cave Canem listerve in 2001–2002. In "Self Portrait as Excess O, O Self Selves," the line "It was black, black took" is borrowed from Gertrude Stein's *Tender Buttons* (Los Angeles: Sun & Moon, 1991, c. 1914).

I. THE BLACK OBJECT

II. DREAM

III. BREAKING BLACK

IV. VERGELIOIAN SPACE

V. IN-AN-IMPRINT

VI. CHRONOPHOTOGRAPHE

VII. THE BLACK BODY

For my Father and Mother

. . . I took myself far off from my own presence, far indeed, and made myself an object. What else could it be for me but an amputation, an excision, a hemorrhage that splattered my whole body with black blood?

—Frantz Fanon
Black Skin, White Masks

Perhaps "race" isn't something that locks us into separate groups. Perhaps it is a state that floats back and forth between us, equally solid and unreal, as if our body and soul were kept apart and, like a kind of Siamese twins, joined only by the thin cord of desire.

—Toi Derricotte
The Black Notebooks

I. THE BLACK OBJECT

ON THE C TRAIN THE BLACK OBJECT PONDERS AMUZATI'S FAMILY EATEN IN THE CONGO

Cut the adults. Huck-um dun the chest,
the deceased lumps.

In the story of edible blacks, hacked and splayed on lattice,
how am I to finish the dishes

with all this dining
in the fields of my instance?

Unremit by browned lung, blisters are blisters, dry by sun,
bucks into bits.

Lattice, works: business is business after all,
but did the Black-Back-Fat deserve its end like the tic I popped?

Sure, if the tic could, it would Visa out of grip.
But, sorry, the sweet, sweet spleens!

In the Magazine, NYT, a teeny pink baby
teeters on the crease of a big palm, cream and light:

Daddy! I am so hungry for some Pyg.

Such hunger, subwayed, the crust on the bittle lack's head —
skin where hair, a spiral spurns beneath flesh.

Ringworm, rung'un, crunk of nap. Mother to baby: *Shut up!*
Don't touch me. Suckcandysuckit. *C'mon now chile'*.

IN PHILADELPHIA THE BLACK OBJECT ROOTS FOR AI SUGIYAMA

Smash the black on a blue
seat back — a white in spite flats

the fly, my arm reclines against
another white's arm hair.

And another opines —
You in the pictures?

Despite Ai Sugiyama cramping
at 7-5, 5-7, 5-5, the whites rise

for the frog-dyke, my Amelie,
not for my Ai.

Is she a friend of yours?
        Yes, in many ways.

Beckoned by perm, cheers
as permanent as diamond

sheen — the rush of the whittle
lights race to the railing

at the end of the match:
Please sign my ball.

Ice packed tight under
her arms, nudged in her thighs

Ai, cooling in the blight —
the fly wiped — and I, lost.

THE BLACK OBJECT GETS KINKY AT HOME

Something crawled
up me and died

a bog
in a taut thought:

I'se a ho,
you know I'se a ho

who's gonna suck
ram it, fork

tongue, my
back fat smacks.

A lazy eye shifts
in gout. Sleep tight

green-itch, the bed
bugs feed

on a hollow leg,
as vacant

teeth in the aviary
fly — my human

figure excised
in the chest

of drawers, hole
in my head

as I rope,
asphyx to zero.

THE BLACK OBJECT'S DEPORTMENT

The black object's phlegm is green in the center of a milky white, which is less of a shock than the look that passes between it and the thin-mustache-of-a-black that waits for its release.

One object waits for the other to form a mouth: it sees pink lips shape to blow waste. A black object, realizing it is being watched, would normally hold a lug in, until the corner.

In fact, it knows, one should spit as little as possible, leastwise upon a floor, but here on a street, approaching a corner, in an instance where one has an audience, the black object lets go.

Lazy lidded eyes vanish into a head. The black object thinks, for its spit, it is met with both expectation and disdain. But one black wanted it from the other. Should spit more often, it thinks.

In a post office line, the black object sees an image of a black, drawn in charcoal, who is supposed to be in a hoodie, but whose upper torso and face emerge like a head in a pod from a bag.

Without a wholly visible head, there is only a flat layer of eyes that float from a sketched surface. Nothing is recognizable beyond the shape of a nose, and the cross hatching around his eyes.

Just when the black object begins to think about that partial black face, how the head is sealed or not sealed in hood or plastic, a Jehri Curled object with a light black baby, screams: "Hurry up!" or "You next!"

Of course, the black object, who hates poor behavior, turns around and casts fast disdain back to the rough black curl who screams, saying to her "Calm down" or "Relax."

Sometimes if one says "Calm down" or "Relax" to a crass black object, that object will operate much like a flag at the end of a wind's tether. Flapping, this is the case: "I'm from L.A!" Looking down to the silent child, the flapper asks, "huh-baby?"

THE BLACK OBJECT'S CATALYST

Your face gets you to a lake, wind chimes, and pear, sliced near a window. This fruit, laid in a spiral and locked to Jarlsberg cheese, staircased in a row with crackers, is yours. In celebration of your face, you think — if you were born to vitiligo lips, and naps, instead of clear skin and curl, what $65,000 per square acre land would you ever get to see? On the drive to this spot, there were llamas in a field, African long-horned steer, goats that look like they've been amputated in half. Pine trees wave in the wind and reflect on the glass table on a deck that extends over the water. On the railing is an abalone's husk. Its meat is gutted, mother of pearl left to catch ash. What if your face were stripped away from this house? Would you remember red: the hummingbird's throat?

THE BLACK OBJECT'S ELASTICITY

It's not as though I felt my body. It's not like I will ever return. In a room, where midnight blue coats the wall, and a black light is bolted to the ceiling, a shirt glows white. A horizon of two bulbs cut the room to a yellow painted galaxy in the corner. Not from daylight or window, I escape fluorescence.

"Fuck You!" "Enjoy your hike back to New York!" "I'm confused." "I'm not even sure why I'm doing this." Answering machines can take such, but how to take being called an *idiot* by an illiterate and to be recalled by that name until three in the morning by this stranger, an alcoholic, a truck driver, who eats steak and beans.

There are ways to evade abuse, some of which have to do with finding a replica of your abuser. One face becomes another face. The red eyes of a lover whose wife is sick, who longs for shemales, who has left his ten acres and lives in a beige box in a trailer park, are replaceable by the right tuft of beard.

I will always remember that flash of his body, where the hips slipped to a redness peeling off the buttock, the rotted nail in the toe, or the teddy bear in the bed the therapist wanted him to cuddle. What I want is to extend from one decay to another — beer breath to yellow teeth to his eyes sunk to hurt.

I feel like a disembodied car part: a pop-up headlight's internal arm that breaks then stabs the radiator, dooming the engine. I know the difference between the engine's injury and the knife in the dish rack, my running as clear as the distance between the moon, running at night, and the tread mill, running in place.

THE BLACK OBJECT'S MEMORY

Blood

In the hotel, there is a bathroom that smells like bleach. Down the hall is a room next to the bathroom, which smells like crack, if this is what crack smells like. In this room, there is a big, black fly on the bed. You're not certain if you remember the fly, there, in that room or in another bed in a different hotel altogether. In either case, the room is hot and small, and the fly, latched to some surface, is as big and black as the blood is dark.

You had no idea he was bleeding. If you knew, you would not have allowed him to take you to this hotel that you can barely remember. You think about saturation, and the way you lifted up the back of his dress shirt. The blood you recall is a thick lacquer on the back of his boxers, a slick, red soak, as though someone stabbed him up the ass. He did what anybody would do after such an attack. He bled.

You knew something was wrong when you saw the small blood stain on the front of the shirt, along its right bottom curve, the dry mark he pulled out of his pants after he must have tucked it in wet. When you saw the source, you said "Oh my God!" and yelled that there was absolutely no way you were going to do anything with him. But you don't want to remember that refusal.

You want to remember when he said, "You know by the eyes." Perhaps you agreed. "Yes, you're right; I knew by your eyes." You could have had him before even looking into them, eyes not longing but lost, not seductive but desperate. It was the way he peered out from around a row of others at the urinals, wide and owlish. It was his tortoise shell glasses, along with the grade of his sweater that placed him from say, Stamford.

He is old and has white hair, which you think was blonde at some point, especially after seeing the stray hairs that shot out of the zipper of his wide wale cords when he faked pissing to shake his dick at you. Despite his uncut, hardening penis that poked out of his pants, there was something else you remember: that he combed his hair against the curl, and how you looked up at him picking the Labrador-or-wife-hair from his sweater like you loved him.

He threw his coat on the hotel floor, but you do not remember the train ride to the floor where the coat lay. What you remember is walking down 42nd street and him putting his arm around you, feeling like you were his and that, from you, he could have anything. "A little blood on the shirt tail is not that bad," you may have thought, but when he pulled his pants down and you saw the bloody boxers, you stopped.

Even though he said, "It's only in the back, you can take care of the front," you pulled away, warned him about the dangers of Hepatitis and HIV, lied when you kissed him on the cheek and said it was not his fault, even though you knew it was his fault to be so carelessly bloody. You cannot stop thinking about the blood in his pants while he waits on the platform for the train back to his home, his Labrador, his wife. You think that he may collapse, that he is bleeding like you imagine the dead to bleed when their bodies give up. You both know what he cannot control, as you watch him enter the train a few cars ahead of you.

Wound

You are not sure if it is quite joy when you see the wound. In fact, you hadn't seen a stab wound, up close, like that since your junior year in high school, when you walked over some kid who was knifed in what appeared to be his spine. "See what happens when you try to come up to Blood Bank?" You felt joy at seeing what came after that stabbing, about walking over his body, about leaving the school on the last day and seeing a boy tapping on the ground with a knife sticking out of his back. You did not think about what sense may have been severed from him as the blade split one disc from another.

So tonight, when you saw this white man, in glasses, mid-30s with an early grey mullet, lift up his Alpaca sweater to reveal the slit in his abs beneath the bloody curtain of his shirt, you said "Welcome to Brooklyn." Your only regret is that you wish the people looking at him were not all black, the only ones cued to the drama: "Yo, that's fucked up." You wish, somehow, that the people partying, drunk on Fulton were not oblivious white girls, or were at least sobered up enough to pay attention to one of their own, stabbed.

Once on this same block, in the middle of the day, there was a corn-rowed black, dragged out of a door a few yards from where this white was stabbed. This man had a similar audience, a bunch of other blacks watching him cuffed, hog-tied and shocked to inert with a taser. "ARE YOU STILL GONNA FIGHT?" The cops pig-pile. They knee as hard as they can into his back. Anyone would resist. It seems natural for any animal to fight when smashed to the ground, a 900,000 volt charge zapped into it: on four, his body a stiff plane on the paddy wagon's floor.

As you look into the ambulance at the white man who got it, is what you feel joy, seeing one man showing his wound and taken to safety while you remember another folded and loaded like living cargo off to jail? There is a dead pigeon smashed in the middle of the street with blood cruising down its leg. You remember someone spraying away blood on the sidewalk, around the corner from your house, where you heard gunfire through the night. In the morning, when you went looking, you learned that blood without a body, blood not washed away by water, coagulates before it dries into a thick, shiny gel.

Toilet

You remember that his beard is thick and nappy. You'd say there was a certain kind of sexiness both in his face and his decision to spread out on the toilet, the thick bud of his black dick in his hands. Pants dropped around his ankles, waiting to suck anyone who came through — red hot in that little shit hole. At least a part of you thinks this. Another part of you thinks that the urinal next to him is like a small boat, in it, a sea of urine.

Even when you piss and look over at his hungry brown lips, you won't feed him. Maybe a part of you wants to feed him, but you can't get over how sickening the floor is, soaked concrete and t.p. anchored by a toilet and his black ass sitting on it, waiting for someone in the Sansom Cinema to fill his mouth as he passes in and out.

Thinking of him is enough to make you want to think about the mountains you drove through from the Advanta Classic to Philadelphia. Where the rubble gave way to dirt off the highway, the hill sloped into exits, smoke stacks, then statues in the periphery — what brings you back from the tennis is the smell, like steel dust shooting up your nostrils, filling you up enough to make you slip your shirt over your face.

16

When you come in to take another piss, you are proud of yourself for getting inside. There was a line of people afraid to go in, because the pot-stuck cocksucker is talking with another motherfucker about nothing at all. It turns out they're both vets. "Can you believe this, he's ex-Army! He knows better than this!" "I'm ex-Navy!" he tells you. "People have they thangs," you import. "My dad was in the Navy too."

"You're gonna get sick." When you say this, you want to lift him up and carry him out to some clean river to soak, watch the rings of filth float from his body. But you also want to piss on him. You imagine his face sprinkled with your vitamin-bright urine. You want to unload on his beautiful black beard what you give to the urinal's mouth, a radiant stream splattering on his dim and tired lips.

II. DREAM

DREAM IN A FAIR

Nellie Olsen's father is my brother.

We are on a ship, a cruise, a tall one overlooking a parade.

There is no water, although there is a street, where a white pony

jumps up on the hips of a clown.

Since the horse is on a leash, it gets snagged and dragged to the floor.

The horse is wet, its mane in the mud and everyone laughs and cheers

at its snag and drag. Alberto is in the dream.

We never hang out, but he's on the deck, looking out at the street.

We're asked to move but we won't.

The M.C. wants us to be in it, to sit in a pink pod.

I wanted to stay put and look out from the couch on a cement balcony.

There is a black man standing at the front of the line.

He's a midget and his teeth are yellow and gapped:

He is short and muscular but covers his body anyway with a costume.

He's about to proceed: as a dragon, or a horse, something

where only his black feet extend from the mane.

You look up at a counter, where a big, bald black, who is your brother,

lets you cut in front of the line. You order turkey

on a plate with potatoes, a cup of water.

In the dream, you are shadowed by time.

Maybe you are out of time, when you encourage Ms. Olsen to buy a book.

Mr. Olsen wants no part of the book, but you look at the slim stacks of twenties

in his wallet and you are turned on that he is your protector too.

You say that book will be worth something in the future.

Maybe it is that future you are rendering in the dream.

In that present, you skip the line and look up at his face to see

your big, bald black brother, now on a bench.

He describes on the phone where he is going —

He says, "I've never been this far."

And you want to say, what do you mean, you've never been this far?

Do you mean North or East?

It is then, you realize, he has no sense of direction.

*

Under a bridge Alfre Woodard is your mother. She's dying of a breathing disorder.

Donald, your brother, died of SIDS before you were born.

You are trying to resuscitate Alfre under the bridge, give her the kiss of life.

She won't revive, but you have an inhaler.

To her aid, others come and she's sitting there under the bridge, looking up.

Left Eye Lopes is angular in the dream; alive, she is in a silver crop-top.

She's a junkie who shows up under the bridge and asks, "Are you _____?"

I can't remember the name, only that I am looking down into Woodard's face.

Another young black woman pulls out a gun that shoots out a dart

full of a tranq that flies through the air at her chest.

Steve Irwin was killed by a stingray barb to the heart today.

He was 44. On the internet, it was black, and he was under the sea.

Stingrays have flat bodies and tails with serrated spines,

which contain venom and can cause cuts and puncture wounds.

The creatures are not aggressive and injury occurs when a swimmer or diver steps on one.

John Stainton, Irwin's friend and producer, said: "He died doing what he loves best

and left this world in a happy and peaceful state of mind."

*

Dawn is reading poems in bed; she is writing what she has already written in blue.

Her writing is blue and white paper.

She is looking at the writing above her poetry. It floats.

The night her father died, I saw his ghost in our hotel room —

first, flashing lights, a yellow, maybe green, like fireflies.

Then, I saw him, a mound, moving under the sheets, a shadow, leaning over to look

at me, turning. The rest is a story of losing my bowels, and running out of the room.

I am meeting Dawn at the movies. I am at one, where I am with my brother.

Dawn becomes Donaldo.

Two more twins look at me from a row in front.

They are older and grey; they say, "Hey. There are twins behind us."

Sense matters.

It matters in this dream, where what you see is the space

between dreams and life.

This seam becomes a question: "What if you returned to the same space,

tried to find the connection between one dream and another?"

Yusef Komunyakaa, I think, said you should not use the word poem in a

poem, but I think in a dream, you must use the word: *dream*.

*

Cliff Drysdale is finally naked in my dream, and he is on a boat.

He's looking out at the audience, pretending to not know he is naked.

His dick is gigantic, and flops to some ten inches, thick and not erect.

There is a pool of people, who float around the cruise ship,

who churn as though in a washing machine.

In this world, one does not need to feel: For instance, a concert

is slightly wet in space, so you don't have to sweat, or cry.

*

The man on Gay.com who looks like my father is above average,

black, grey, nappy beard, something about his smile, white and easy —

He's offended when I tell him I am cute. "What happens," he asks, "when you

are no longer cute?" "No," I tell him. "I'll only be older, and less cute."

I tell him, what I see and hear makes me cute. I want to say *acute*.

*

Before bed, I remove the pillows from my deck furniture.

There is a leaf-bug on the deck.

I've never seen a live insect, so green and rare.

"Rare" is what the man who looks like my father says we are:

Two blacks who are whole, he clarifies.

I still have nightmares —

The leaf-bug struggled in the bright lights on the deck as I closed the tennis can

over its body. In a dream, a dolphin is in my big duffle bag.

I'm not sure how it got in my bag, or what airport I am at, or where I am going.

I am trying to remember a song in the dream. "For Once In My Life . . ." It is all

I can remember — Karmen remembers the song and sings the whole thing.

*

Pattern organizes trauma, and so does speed.

We are singing as we walk, holding hands, remembering the song as it blurs.

There is a big, black homeless man, who is walking down the street towards the fair.

He cuts off the space between me and Erica.

He is on her side, before I jump between the two of them.

The big, black homeless man gives me a quick, light punch on the arm.

The leaf-bug has shit in the tennis can, and when I try to remove it, I can't.

It does not recognize up from down, in from out, air from the bottom.

I took the label off so that it could not hide.

When I tried to let it go, it did not respond, clinging to the plastic with its little claws.

In the dream, the dolphin is making noises, and kicking.

My bag is gigantic, filled with this shifting, and in it, the dolphin is singing.

It wants to escape. I forgot it was in my bag, but now I've called over an attendant.

He is Indian, I think, or some other kind of Asian.

"I can't find my ticket. . . ."

This is what I tell him, although I know my ticket is in my pocket.

The bag of clothes shifts. Its outline is clear.

The dolphin bulges about and flops around.

If I shake it, maybe it will shut up.

When I shake the tennis can, the bug flips.

Its shit sticks, small black dots.

Last night it went without food, water or air.

Today, I'll release it into the sun.

I hope the bug is snatched up by a bird.

Yesterday, there was a field of black birds that dotted the green grass.

I'm not sure — if what I saw on the end of the bug was the stinger or the sex organ.

In any case, whether reproduction or destruction,

I feel more guilt than power.

In the morning, the men are pounding outside my window.

Truth is, only when it snows here is it ever really quiet.

Project after project: What about this misplaced fear?

Suzanne, the woman above me, lives in fear.

Hers is random: Will the house burn down when I am teaching?

I'll back up my work, take it with me.

Will a bear attack me at night?

*

I hate animals: maybe this is why I trap the leaf-bug.

It gives me a way of containing fear.

Dallas said, "What do you think I would say if you asked me?"

Before I asked him, I put the can in the freezer.

I wanted to numb the leaf-bug. It was grappling to the plastic top.

I was afraid that when I stuck it in the window, it would fly back and sting me.

When I was at Djerassi, I ran with a knife in my pocket and a stick in my hand.

There was a dog around the corner, where the grounds keeper said:

"Everywhere is safe."

Out of the freezer, in the can, the leaf-bug is encased in a shroud of white mist.

It is stuck to the top.

I've killed it. I should have let it fly away.

It plopped out of my sight, as I let it fall from the can, frozen to the earth.

People who torture and kill animals make great murderers, but I do feel guilt.

Perhaps this is the guilt of the killer.

Dallas says, "It gave its life for you, and you

won't even go out there to find it?"

When I scan the brown ground, where I thought I'd see green leaves, I see it.

There it is lying frozen on the ground, twitching, half thawed.

"It has no protection." This is what Dallas said, and now I see it's true.

It's too cold to fly, but nothing eats it. It blends in.

No, really, it was gone.

*

Should Irwin's final moments be shown?

Yes he'd want it: 64%

No, too morbid: 36%

Will this be the end of similar wildlife shows?

No, they will stay: 93%

Yes, they're too dangerous: 7%

The other day, I wanted to draw a picture of a girl that flashed in my head,

while walking down the street.

I imagined her long black hair and eyes blacked out:

Black as the black in the black of black.

So when I went to look for the video footage

of the barb that lanced into Irwin's heart,

his body, a struggle in sea, some floating paralysis,

some death, I found a mock site — my click,

then a guttural screech,

the eyes of the girl

come to life.

III. BREAKING BLACK

THE BREAKER'S POSE

I will kneel to him.
—Caliban

It passes, from head spin
to spun Cotton. Pink, rosacea excess,

the skin waits to glut. *Oil.*   I whisper
when I choose.

In that hiss: [   ]

Not Caliban, but alley born.   Rotate.
Strike:[   ]Floor work, not *shufflin'*

        Kick: Cull the skull.

THE BREAKER'S PERFORMANCE

Will wine and cheese glut my art,
kill my pop-locking arms?

Will it de-coon my continence,
make me a *better* black?

Had this been the rat poison
under my stove, I would've left it alone.

Had this been lumpia, pancit, a *food* song,
you'd give me an island.

If I leaped into the arms of the first white
suit and broad chest I saw, I might sink.

This last and desperate arc by spine is no
nigger dance, no-blaxo-blessed-be.

        I spin: my back bores into the floor.
        I tear out my song, not yours.

BREAKER'S MOVE

In the Twist-O-Flex,
the chin follows the Egyptian
hands whip-around:

He pops. He pops good.

Shackles snap —
The torso torques.

Sense

       breaks.

Do not utter a corner.

Watch the spot. A head
looks out
the body's
form.

BREAKER'S FORM

It is not left out on the road:

Burnt. A Burner. Tag it.

Seize sight: My house has a blue minivan

and a red Porsche in the garage,

a porch and yard.

I am wide and fat: my endless reproach,

palm between oil stains on cardboard.

ARIEL'S FREEZE

Has it broke yet,
does my arm stink?

Do I Flame Amazement?
Do I not creep

here, my head

shaken?

In the city, where

Body Lock, Tick.

the towers crash into a hole,

I do *a 1990.*

Break the black body —

        Up
Rock

— Break the brown skin.

We don't need no water . . .

Let this newish, *thing.*

IV. VERGELIOIAN SPACE

VERGELIOIAN SPACE IV: THE BULIMIA METHOD

do do. [1]

Was thinking about voice today, while practicing on the train ARIEL's
singing to Prospero in the Tempest and love the part that go, go:

. . . The burden. Hark, Hark!
(Burden, dispersedly)Bow-wow.
The watch dog bark.
(Burden, dispersedly) Bow wow.
Hark, hark! I hear
The strain of strutting Chanticleer,
Cry cock a diddle dow.
(Burden, dispersedly)
Cry Cock a diddle dow. . . . [2]

    Upon singing, I was flattered to find out that my students said *I SOUNDED
LIKE JUSTIN TIMBERLAKE*! And I really gave it to them near the end with a
lilting thing I learned to do with my singing voice by listening, obsessively, to the
whole of Tracy Chapman for the last half of my life. . . .

Cry/ cock/ a diddle/ doooo
ooohhh ooohhhhh . . . cock a diddle, dooo ohhh ohhhhh . . .

Which, of course, is less important than the tone of Ariel's voice, but singing taught
me a little something about blackness and *being* as a collective sight and about my
trust in the word *fun*. [3]
    Without my mother: I have to ask her how to be more Sycorax-sexy later on
this afternoon. She wants me to come along. She has a date with her very elegant
editor, which means tea and lots of paper at XXXXX. She's working on a piece about
the dance company Pina Bausch and the Sublime or something — more riffing on
Wet, Walrus bodies as anti-castration narratives; she's deft and crafty that way.

43

Carmelina, my mother, says one of her secrets to effective critical readings (of plays or the ballet) is to make sure to bring toothpicks to every performance, to always wear easily removable shoes, and to make sure to communicate (if possible) by VOICE one's enjoyment. We once got kicked out of some SWEDISH Avant-garde version of the Nutcracker because my very tiny mother threw her very big, expensive day bag at the lead dancer who was cursing the audience in broken English. Something like:

"FFUEWECK FUUUK FUCKKERS

FWEEK

FUUUCKKK UUU FUUICKK
NUT CRACK."

Ariel's voice is like my mother's AFTER she agrees to write for publications or to send things to editors, or to simply meet with them. She is such a good schmoozer, all truth and elegance. Ariel's voice is like my mother's, the moment she decides to speak without having to resort to such drastic anti-communicative measures like violence, despite it working, for her, most of the time.

Though, unlike ARIEL, my mother is hardly slave-like and refuses to cull an audience that cannot relate to her tactics in isolation.

A more simple answer is that this space (in where you read) is a place for a hydra-collective voice despite one's own obsessions, or because of them, as a thematics toward loss or loss of control over one's overt poetic practices.

At least that is what my mother would say.

Or it's like a mirror.

I could care less, but care deeply about foreign matters, new modes, obsessions and have been thinking about "cull and repose" not call and response for the last few months in my writing and reading. [4]

And now, what would a thematics after (gas p) loss, silence, hiding, hindrances, gaps, cuts, slits, vacancies, holes, (ga sp) desecrations, ah-loves, olives pose or manifest or re-pose or (g asp) anti-manifest? [5]

Now what is this, if not an overt thematics? The idea, here, is that recognizing failure, the failed, the exhausted is to embrace WRECKEDCOGNITION, something after the spirit of my mothers thinking in her novel, "Maghug Baboy Bilang I Nag," a wonderful village tale that ends in basic hand-to-hand combat between some VERY angry darkies.

To go under, to go down, to avoid, to sink, to slip, to see the idea of confronting the head-on collision in being found.

What a shame. I am lost all the time, lost just enough to know that this loss is part of an aesthetic economy that evolves me in more evolutional orders than I can eat, but I keep stuffing my face, eating with my mouth open and vomiting like a good bulimic.

I am writing a poetry toward the bulimic!

I am writing notes to all casual bulimics!

I am healthy AND had for lunch today the most amazing chicken salad and seven grain masterpiece made by a woman that I felt I had to charm in order to get the bigger plate that featured the slippery chips and big VLASIC Pickle.

Notes:

[1] After Imani Tolliver's *eeeek*. And Mendi Obadike's *SEE*.

[2] Stephen Orgel's edition is fascinating.

[3] In Wayne Koestenbaum's *Cleavage*, he writes about *fun*, or promises to write more about *fun* in another context BESIDE (or maybe besides) his brilliant shopping for a new PRADA suit. I, myself, am trapped by Calvin Klein and sometimes Hugo Boss. Prada, not yet. I do have fellowships to win. WIN!

[4] "Cull and Repose" is from my mother's first novel, still untranslated in English: *Maghug Baboy Bilang I Nag*.

[5] Am thinking about the moment between feeling and the written text, action and the "said" thing, the "felt" thing, the grasp is the point, but then what is the gasp or the breathing that Mendi and I love to do with one another?

For me, the point is to explore fear, as well, as Mendi is doing by breaking apart language and pointing us in new directions and modes through which to spear space. SPEAR! I haven't read the Laura Riding piece in FENCE so closely, but want to return to it, directly, like I want to return to Langston Hughes' *The Big Sea*! Hmmmmmm. His BIG anti-biography?

Always Yours and Ever Faithful, Vergelio

VERGELIOIAN SPACE V: CALIBAN X

Re-monster: Once, I wrote a short response piece at a summer youth camp called *Macular Degeneration*, which was about an old dying white man's dead mother. [1]

I ended up going home with him, somewhere in Conn. (and always) next to some giant freshwater pond. But before we got to all the air, I thought: *If he wanted, he could shoot me in the head and push me out of his big car on whatever stretch of highway we were on.*

At some point in the night, he told me his mother lost her ability to see straight forward, hence her macular degeneration, which developed further until she died.

I loved thinking of her growing peripheral and permanent new sight.

I can't make the direct connection between that and the poetics suggested in a note Mendi gave me about the fun in turning out the parenthetical ( ) into a)(, which occurs sort of like the curve into a waist. Even though I aspire toward that particular hiplessness, no waist and a single line for everything I do. [2]

I was thinking earlier today about certainty: I was reading xx, the other day and got xx. If I am xx, I will be seen as xx, and then my xx of a life will matter to xx.

Now figuring that out gets unduly complicated by: But I am an xx, who chooses to write as an xx, and that xx is loved by xx, XX and maybe by yy and YY, who all love me.

Further, they made me XX but never yy, only some perverse version of (our) xyXY fantasy, which is always a matter of Race, which is after all a bibliographical construction of being celebrated as the ever recognizable me in print but not in SPACE.

Mow down the MODE!

So being pushed out of a moving car in the middle of no-where means much more if there is NOT a bullet lodged in my brain. Or, it means even more so, if the bullet passes through the head. Maybe it wouldn't hurt as much as I hit the highway.

More directly, maybe the role of the victim might be either less interesting sans bullet or as the living, it, rolls about (out of CONTROL) at 65 MPH or faster.

It was dark.

I was drunk.

I deserved him, then.

I suppose what I am getting at is that I find my mother very frustrating to deal with. She is the one who is so out of control:

Carmelina was 35 minutes late to her meeting with the editor. She said that she was intentionally late because she thought she should arrive in style, which for her means NOT HUNGRY. She stopped into some chocolate shop and bought a pound of truffles or something and ate half and was sugar rushed.

She said: "Ronaldo, I felt sensual."

By that time the editor was pissed, but was eased over by the other half pound of chocolate my mother offered him, all boxed and untouched. Despite her kindness and thoughtfulness, the editor was not willing to accept the direction of her current draft. The main question, as she explained it to me — and this I think was a problem not with the writing but its verve — was and is: How can Pina Bausch use a walrus as a vehicle for one's black suffrage. How does a walrus crawling across a stage equal the pure pain involved in psychic castration?

Well, to me it seems so simple. Race is all made up. None of it exists: the language, the voice, the stance, the delivery, the celebration, the connery, the cytoplasm, the coins that have my head on them, the cat, the re-memory, the whole big lot. But the pain is as evident as all these silly terms we make up for our salvation.

See: xx.

But of course, this sight line (xx gets exposed. xx sees.) is not binocular but macular, not direct, nor does it assume any direction other than the one suggested in turning the parenthetical OUT, which is about re-creating a space for extra-communal discourse. To me, this is simply free-ing.

But then, as it seems, the big xx is one tough motherfucker to bypass. See: XX wants that obscene part of the little xx not the fat but the phat, not the back but the black, not the spoon as SHANK but the nuuk nuoook nuoogah, as xxxxxx, which is such a horrid wall to be against. [3]

Lordee knows, I wish I could be a better performer.

Sadly and Yours until the end, Vergelio

Notes:

[1] Unpublished, it, in fact, is in a box somewhere, stored on a 3x5 floppy (disc) someplace and can only be accessed by a computer that refuses to decompose in some landfill.

[2] Of course, I prefer no curves at all, unless they be the //: This angle, the cryptographic slant into figurative space is toward a poetics of internal excess: How I refuse to comment other than by cryptographic gesture, or by yet another sentence. But I would KILL to be Kate Moss, Rori Abernethy, and especially JAMES KING!

[3] I was thinking about going to read G. Brooks's "The Wall" for a more fair and open analysis, but had to get to class, uptown where I took the 2 train to 110th street which left me outside in Harlem! instead of at Columbia, on the other side of the world. Something was wrong there. In Harlem, bodies were out in the sun near buildings of great brick. They were sunning, relaxed, chatting. Driving Ivy Caps. There were no sub-humans in sight, and I did not realize what was wrong until I detoured back with my 63 dollar Metro Card into the subway only to rewind out onto Broadway. I ran into a familiar teeming stream of working fruit-sorting-blacks near Labyrinth books where I bought: Fanon's *Black Skin, White Masks* and a book on performance/poetics edited by Charles Bernstein and another book starring Fred Douglas and Ida B. Wells. But more importantly, I cried on the train while reading about *be be*, the dead slave boy guiding Harriet's nymphish follower to freedom in Faith Ringgold's *Aunt Harriet's Underground Railroad in the Skyyyyyyyyyyyyyyyyyyyyyyyyyyyyyyy*.

VERGELIOIAN SPACE VI: OPEN LETTER TO FAITH RINGGOLD AND MICHELE WALLACE

WHAT I AM DOING IS PUTTING UP A FENCE. IT IS HIGH AND TALL. IT

went to class today. was about composition. was about purpose. was not about
originality. was about purpose. was about composition. was about thinking about the
purpose. was not about what one is doing, and not originality [1]

IS IN EFFECT, A WAY OF ME DEMARCATING SPACE IN AN OTHERWISE

went to class today and heard a mother, Faith Ringgold talk about the surface of
cotton, the suffocating surface of the mouth, and I was dumb. I am sad, and admitted
it to think of what to say. went to the cotton fields in her *America Series*, not the
sequence, was waiting in the corner:

CROWDED ROOM. THESE NOTES ARE PUBLIC. THESE NOTES ARE ALL

you should not try to be original, just think of the purpose. (F.R.)[2]

MY ORIGINAL AND PUBLIC SALVATION. THIS FENCE IS MADE OF THE

went to class today. went to class and said, I read this on the train, *Aunt Harriet's
Underground Railroad* — went there and showed the booooooooooooooooooook to
Faith. shesignedinblackpermanentink. went to the underground railroad and started
thinking about the things that I would photograph had I had a camera: black matter
poured out of the wall. the light that coats the surface of the bottom of the subway
terminus. an orange rolls into a puddle of water into the gutter.

WOOD THAT I SAW TONIGHT ON A CROSS OF A MAN WALKING DOWN THE

went to class today and learned about seeing through the eyes of another artist, an
older wiser one: I can say ancestor without embarrassment or shame, not thinking

wise but in the spirit of PLAY. What is the spirit of play if not here? went to class
today and learned about seasoned laughing because I hear it, and do it and hear it.

STREET. JESUS'S BACK. IN MY CITY, BLACKS SCREAM ABOVE ME. ONE

saw a new series today and pieces and pictures of a studio hidden in New Jersey.
*wanted my own studio and the others, they tried to stop it, and then the high fence
came up and then the studio.* (F.R.) have to think about being in Provincetown and
not having them get me at my then new home; I did not want to have to deal with it
there. went to class today to bury my own process. [3]

BLACK YELLS ABOVE ME AT THE OTHERS. I AM UTTERLY ALONE, YET

went to class today and thought about composition, after, about the endless living
of that space, the way in my dream the whole of it opened up like a wedge. went
to the edge of the light and tried to write feverishly in the fat li'l notebook I bought
today. went to class today to learn more about freedom; yes, I am free, and look into
the mirror of this making as a gift. wonder about my voice, and being original, less.
wonder who you are in this space? [4]

WITH OTHERS, I AM ANOTHER WHO IS BLACK. AFTER WE LEAVE, I WILL

went to class today and thought about what this means. . . . *that if you learn about
composition from the master, you may never learn to compose, but if you think
about how to deal with space.* went to class today and heard Faith Ringgold, a
painter, talk about learning, first, by the white, european masters and then to learn
about composition by learning how to deal with SPACE. was the evening's pure
revelation. the return. thinking about form and formality. this, now, is a chapter of
my dissertation, the first steps of a poem, my book, the slow, hard, long-black-easy-
shiny path that is not lain before me or you. [5]

THINK OF US, TOO, AMONG THEM. IF I COULD, I WOULD HAVE LAWYERS TO

went to class today, sad, and to sleep sad, and after having to tell another student that I would help her get the object that she wanted, not roll it out to her upon command. I wanted to feel free, to feel not like Caliban, not like the sing-monster without language, not the spewing thing, not the thing saying yes, and then the praises, not that thing singing and singing: what comes out of the driftwood but my own heavy voice?

PROTECT ME AND EVERYTHING THAT I BUILD. BUT I HAVE YOU.

Notes:

[sinceiamthinkingaboutmakingfencesandthesearetransparentirealizeicannotsendthisand

[1] I had a dream. The dream was of me, dreaming about fried chicken as a night composition. In my stupor, I am looking at the shape and box of a composition, which is a series of collapsed black frames, bouncy, flexible, porous, and then the intersections of liquid and fried fat.

ihavedecidedtoletthisgo,thenthehopeisthatithelpsmethinkaboutwhatonecreates.ifnotaholea

[2] I cannot sleep, because the phone is ripping me out of sleep. I cannot sleep because I did not run tonight, nor lift weights, nor break. I did not lift tonight, myself, did not float, and realize that my swimming is like my flying.

desecrationrequiresanintertextualquotesosaygwendolynbrooks,andthehardsmellofgarlic

[3] In class today, Faith Ringgold talked about a new series of paintings after *The French Series* and *The American Series* and about the architects who built a space around her house. There are slaves in the portraits that are bound by black, chunky shadows that circulate like ghosts. I loved looking at the eyes of the people in her new and old work.

floatingthroughthehouse.iwonderifthisisthebeginningortthefinishingtext.thattobeignoredor

[4] I've been feeling this intense sadness in the act of writing, and sending into silence. the idea of an open letter has always fascinated me. My unpublished ground zero manuscript, *Open Letter to the Con Edison Man Near My Body*, was an exercise of talking to the man, but what about him talking to me? What does that composition look like?

tobereadinprivateismeaningfulinanyway.myhopeisthatyouarereadingthisandiam winningtoo

[5] I loved hearing Faith Ringgold talk about composition, because it made me value her even more, and made me think about her daughter, one of my teachers who teaches me about space and lets me have it feels the way into space. I am lucky.

thatweallareinsomeway,wallace,ringgold,wilson,carmelina,thepilipinesiamfromno wherus

With Great Love, Admiration and Respect,

Vergelio

V. IN-AN-IMPRINT

CONSTRUCTION OF A BLACK POETIC SELF IN FOUR NARRATIVES

1. A Narrative

Between memory, muscle and fat is a poetics out of a black, pleather satchel full of photos.

A few shots are of my father, teaching tennis to a group of men in Guam, most of them white. Everyone is wearing white. And there is Leland Doane, who is all chest hair and long hairy arms with a sloped forehead, who had a wife named Phong, who my parents said had gone crazy.

When Leland Doane sent us some of our belongings to Tennessee from Guam, the pots and pans were missing.

When his wife suffered a brain hemorrhage, he came to Tennessee, alone. Too trusting, my father let Leland Doane drive a U-Haul full of our furnishings from Tennessee to California, and of course, we had again, by this man, been robbed.

Not looking at the photos, but instead, to think of them, reveals this action:

My father leans forward, knees bent, black mustache, loose skin, afro, leg out, a lunge mimics where the imagined ball meets the racquet.

2. Narrative and Disruption

I have never seen a trace of fat on my mother's body. The idea of fat on her, pure impossibility. When I was a boy, I remember

To write between something else I recall, or after what is triggered from memory is a place where my narrative disrupts itself, again. To identify with the fractured self, the process of the it forced apart by language, again, is where the self explodes out of the text not by narrative as story — one act — but more simply as found photo — another act — as forming poetic. Becoming through narrative, or becoming by reaching lazily under a bed to find something valuable, or again, more simply, digging under one object and stumbling on meaning asks: Does this narrative begin in a black hole? Does it create another diasporic space? Is this space black? Is it *a* black?

driving in a car with my father and brother, riding beside her as my father kept the speed trained to her marathoner's pace.

3. *[Narrative]*

In a box, my father's torso is
in a white thermal rib top
(my
own face leaning in to find
my face
in his black shiny skin)
between my mother,
a then fattish filipino girl,
with a cinched waist is
the speed
at which she trained
to run off
excess flesh.

4. *One Narrative Between Another*

My mother, in another photo has arms like Martina Navratilova (circa 1985) her legs

The bend of an elbow around her daughter's stomach, her long black hair behind her, in a ponytail under a hat. This photograph is what I found, once, and now remember and need to write out of and onto the satchel's dust, one layer of sense into another.

boomed out in muscle, her arms like thin cannons, clutched around my sister.
She wore

This is an act of writing into the fear of fat, which is not about fat but a metaphor for
running away from fat into more deliberate forms of excess. This decadent athletics is of a
particular moment, the choice to say what I want is to create one version, after another, of a
constantly imagining self.

a tennis hat that flopped a shadow over her smiling mouth. Her skin was burnt
brown by

Each shot (photograph, point, poem, sentence) my memory, truncation, embrace, deferral,
a poetics, is not writing out of or into, but through the center of whatever I mark to be the
current state of what is the deliberate gesture in:

It is impossible to say who I am.

the sun. There she was, dark and almost as muscular as I am now.

IN-AN-IMPRINT

1.

Loss: in being far too often, the site of it, you may find it in a severed branch outside your window. Your plant, a surface, cut. Once treeing itself up through cement, the great leaf-memory is gone. What occurs, a thin red stem, new sprout, an aphid's wing.

2.

Forge from this, your body against stone, your hand up against a pillar, you pregnant, thin and a shadow. Photographed in Kordofan, you are at work, moving rocks. Signaled with the inanimate: an end, an edge in a world where you are the limit.

3.

Hone a love of an art. Or an arc. An arc of light. A burst that brights above a sidewalk you walk. Your own language against that flash. Pick how to say it, a word. Utter, to catch the thing that shoots in your periphery, then out of sight.

4.

Or maybe you are more athletic; your body sweats from what you build. Dance near your laptop. Write, out of breath. You are like a fly that escapes, or one who dies as it flees into what it loves, its obsession, its moving, its ceaseless want.

5.

No north star. Be like a slug taking salt. Not the pain. No cutting. No crack, nor weed. No thing but the mesh of your dissolving. The bubbling. Or the body dried up and left: e.g. *a memory* — a firecracker in a wall — POP! — an animal's yellow guts ooze.

6.

Feel. Unconscious. Un-Make. Sense, and line it as you wish — repel, rebel. Trust in what you hear: words, and even the sounds you remember, the mumble of strangers — a bus breaks, glass — the speed of a train flying down a track, for miles, your freedom.

7.

Be quiet. Resist a blues. Be-the optic in b OP. Cacophone, harmony. Stir fry Soul-Food. Swallow a saxophone. No sonnet to prove your eloquence. Twist, braid, dye, press, doo-rag. Run away. Clear ice, pomade Slick-Rick. Or don't. Run. Run to.

8.

Your block will get knocked. It's only a matter of when. Or how and what speed it will come, off. Despite throwing your hands in the air, waving as though you don't care, someone does. Someone will. You will catch blow after blow, and have to make, sense.

9.

Expect what you see to vanish. Keep saving until your coins burst out of the jar. Stay — thin, warm, fat, loose — to wear what you wish. Confuse the state of the face that blacks you in, an eternal marker of place. Mark. Explode the seen.

10.

Niggery, black a lot — brown — high colonic. e.g. 2. *a memory*: One of us opened fire up on this train in 1993, shooting whites. A black, splattering. Would you crouch? Will you return to stare back at this body, caught, volumizing in blood?

SELF PORTRAIT A: *ALIMENTARY*

for Abner Louima, beaten and tortured by NYC Police

trees spread hard
as the legs of a roach

thorned up in a low sky
an exhaustion

like the fear of a body
or it as a rubber suit or belt

in the bog bilge
pulled across the moss

a smashed wheel barrow
in the brain fractures

into a twitting chameleon
begging for it

a plunger in the bowel

i have come for the knocked out teeth
the blood the shit mouth

my face bears down
in the asphalt path up hill

lying there a giant
Venus at dawn

lain down to light up
the ants gnawing

back into earth

SELF PORTRAIT AS EXCESS O: *O SELF SELVES*

four white lights bleed

or black hole as the point of brilliance

in the heart   a white hole pounds

out a mode of lightning   grasp to screen   bug by day

determinate by mist   a pile of trees

a pile of trees   a phone call with a stranger's photos in a box

it makes no sense   it is unclear   it has no chance

it is rotten steak   blacken it

i will cut you   a rage of meat   of decadent cards

a brutal end: Ruby Jean Johnson   dead   slain   slain

by crack addict   an alien by alien in the rendering

a wisp of useless hair   a tank top in

harlem: the lazy eyed thief cousin

dumb by weed   dumb by hot dog and cheese

dumb by adoption   dumb by dumb

way of seeing the headlights on the semi open

a whir of opposition in the homophone

oscilloscope   frame this moment where obsession is badness:

be bad   the glutton says: *It was black, black took.*

next: reburn your face   re wash your head

black   the downy lip of a freak

a flower syndrome   pass on   the black heart

will my body break down the bile's impossible confusion:

i am your autograph

why my eye   a black point speaks   obsidian

mouth slit by two crows: their song is dead

your hard daddy is left   fat and round   with a fat and round brain

i am hot all the time   sometimes be girl

trying to make everything pretty

or a girl   that flower girl

burning girl   a lady   a lass

big bird is a yellow miss who wish to big beak crack open your head

know why a love poem really in the urticaria   why i learn to carry ya

the arch over the sky   in the rasp

of a conversation   a conversion   i am ready

to kick in your face

a vacuum to accept this hate

racing cock wild movements in the fold

name them: collard or   collard green   col lard   be a fat ass

be a fuck face   a fucked face on a pillow   swallow   swallow in the brain

swallows   swallow to be swelled in a harrowing wood   looking up   with not light

VI. CHRONOPHOTOGRAPHE

CHRONOPHOTOGRAPHE

Helmet in the tundra, brylcreem and fixed — boxed hip bone and cock pumped, bow down to it. His hands, like large cages, arthritic fuck toys. Sycophant, the brain deadens, as in confusing effluvium for effusia. Nostrils flare, an ill wind. I lick a mass of glucosamine. I want his wire glasses on before he fucks. Makes him soft: scarecrow arms pulled back by wild marionette cords. The pink bulbous head over which I slip. Old spiced, meat, I swim in his tit hair and crawl over his milky paunch.

Fig. 1.

Big and strong, 19, Vast, 6-foot-10, 240, but a deeply troubled soul, a black jock is a trauma pocked on the glutes where the old muscle splits. A fiscal eye — at the Townhouse, one investment banker is a bee keeper. He's hot with his head and torso sealed by netting. Like the sleep induced insects, a row of stick bodies span the painting above the bed. Two gold watches pillow on wrists that lie back. Pounded by a smooth and skinless boy is a sunning crock. Lube and a towel strewn — a feeding frenzied chicken digs into its last hutch.

Fig. 2.

When I said how easy I could strangle him, right then, he believed I would. A naked principal should not be uncut and weak as pinkie clay. His cigar should flip back into the sunset. For head, I in excess, find an orgy box: in a mirror, three white rhinos fuck like Venus Hottentots. Breath streams through one slit, as though one animal. While tracks boot mark the snow, melt down to ice, and freeze like fish bones, Kong's angry pellets steam up the rivulets. Ape, I am preoccupied, a frozen heart fires into his body like fetid flour.

Fig. 3.

Ill, a big black heart. Cells river in the bituminous hole. I make a substance, an alloy epiphany the same scene with three barreled and hairy chested men not fucking, really, but making sounds. Gesticulating. Sure, their cocks touch, but they don't penetrate. What does man A hope to touch? B wants me. C is the owner of a big fat hand. In the *largest older men porn site on the internet*, sheep leap over fences at the bottom margin of the *New Pics* gallery. *Pic 7*: I am touched by the inalienable piss slit and perineum, agape.

Fig. 4.

Sandy blonde continental cut by Xeroxed eyes and there's enough of the stone gut to peep the muscled heart — a valley of twisted trees gore through the snow. Pic 3: The scanned trophy's gold body is a rectored swimmer. About 57, a man is couched on a quilt whose arrows point between his spread thighs. Cry-laughing at his own dick, it's as though he thinks: how can I be attached to so much? The curve of it, like wild game shocked from the marsh. The window blasts white on his flat sternum.

Fig. 5.

If I hurl myself down over it, force it in and think, I am the vortex, itself, who should hold the loss? If I raid the hard and dead object, and after, skid across the frozen snowed lake to freedom, I am the uncontained, one plate bore of porcelain's silence. Forcing a coma in the abyss, I want one artifact, the uncut stump from his body. Savage or wily trauma, I want that thing — to swallow it. Who will taste the salt in my mouth? Feel the endless rip of the sun, its yellow light forced against the petrified pine.

Fig. 6.

HERMAN THE GERMAN IS DEAD

after Herman the German, Porn Star

Herman hung a horse shoe on his hard cock.
    And though eager to suck, he let himself

go.
                             In one movie,
he breaks into a house and finds a magazine

on a work bench, where large, fat, white men
like him, near seventy

fuck.

Rubs his jump suit crotch. (He wears
a handle bar moustache.)

Flips through what
for him is a book of mirrors.

Before he pulls it out, I expect the uncut mass
to do more than answer

what I know about myself,
that if I saw him

                             at a train station
                             or in a park
                             or on 14th street
                             or at the Grand
                             Hyatt Hotel urinal,

of course, I would

kneel.

REMEMBERING THE DEAD

Thinking of Herman's death is not a lament
but an act of obsession,

akin to a set of prepositions: in, or on, or at.
Locating the death

outside of a stupid question,

I ask BigChet: Was it AIDS?
No, it was age.

                    In the middle of memory, I am
keen,

know, that to want anything in excess is
part of a map I set

myself against (Herman's big white body, silver
hair, his face):

If my body is brown and muscular, my face
heavy, jaw boned, dimpled and full

of perfect teeth.

My eyes, vacant.

If I am well veined and long fingered,
fast and agile,

he is dead.

RETINA

I can see clearly now the rain is gone.

A song: Why does thinking of him
make a plane

in my head,
plywood, splinters.

A fire wall:

I want to build one in my own body,
a wall so high and bright that no one

may peer through
to the other side.

Last night, I went hunting for old white men.
Came home empty handed.

Had I known Herman the German
was dead,

I would not have turned on
the *Old Man and the "C,"*

The C stands for Cunt.
I want one. I want a cunt.

The word is one letter and an extra "T"

away from *cum*.

I *came* while watching Dick Nasty's
white and blonde orange bushed cock

die on a beautiful woman's mouth.

WANT

Herman the German is my lover.

Herman the German lives in a ranch house that I visit.

In his house, he wears a jump suit with nothing underneath.

Herman the German saying my name is not as important as when he says *damnit* on the phone, twice, which leaves a double thrush of air in my ear.

Herman the German drinks coffee like I like it, dark, with fat free milk and no sugar.

Herman the German sips it all morning as he thinks.

Herman the German teaches me how to build emotional firewalls.

No-one shall cross them, not even him.

Not even Herman the German who is large and white.

Herman the German is Aunt Jemima's unconscious twin.

They are twinned because I buy her syrup and like watching her face as I drown my pancakes with her liquid life.

Herman the German is filmic.

I want to fuck Herman the German, but never will, because he's dead.

HERMAN THE GERMAN IS ALIVE!

Dear Reader,

Do you remember the scene in *Pearl Harbor*, where Ben Affleck is about to crash into the ocean and black oil spits on his face? Do you remember how he shoots his gun through the cockpit window to escape?

He died. He did not swim to shore. That was the pilot's selfish ghost you and the audience were forced to watch. You wish he came back. You wish he loved her. You wish he didn't sink to the bottom of the sea.

Dead,

Herman the German

VII. THE BLACK BODY

BRUTAL END

. . . Cops say 81-year-old Ruby Jean Johnson was raped and then slain by a
crack addict last year in her Harlem Apartment . . .
        —Daily News

In the photo, my hair blurs into an ovum of ash,
skin smooth as a girl's. The flash finds my eyes,
two tiny white grids, lips betongued

as though I lisp. Punctum:
I am refuse, my tank top killed.
Killed again, I am

                    in the A&P, white eyes glow from a
                    mug coon eyed up to the energizers.

                    Dead Batteries?

O helpless mute of the tile and flooring. With what to pull
you through the screen of my raped and slain face —

a shovel,
an oyster shucker?

An anagram: *Don't let the black cat in. He can't let himself out.*

            That boy burnt up his grandma.

If our bodies are hieroglyphs,
I sing of the charred robe,
the skins steaming catharsis.

(Avoid savage relatives. Buy a flame retardant robe.)

O vacuities. If we are endless holes,
I claim the discordant. I claim the pigsty.
The split subject.

I claim incommunication.
Not the steel filed down to black dust,
I am the anvil's bow and flat surface:

my frames gape, as though skin
ripped open like a face burned by iron
for being beautiful.

I want the spell of cellophane, its clear preserve,
gold hoops sealed in the glass door knob.

Once, on a spoon, I boiled baking soda and water
until they caked, and bore a substance:

in the singed metal, gesticulates

the snow blower —
drives snow into snow,
wind convulsing to matter.

THE SEMAPHORE

Where the body builder wants pecs,
"Dr." Reinaldo Silvestre stuffs in silicon

breasts, videotapes it and jams
a copy in his patient's mouth.

On the loose in South America, he leaves behind a string
of scalpeled off lips and sewn shut eyes, a trail

John Walsh, avenger of missing children and
gynecomasts alike, cannot follow.

Leeza, the talk show host, summons to the stage
a dead girl's mother.

It doesn't matter how she looks, a print blouse, fat, fried hair:
The blow up photo of her baby blonde daughter

is what counts (raped, roped to bricks, then tossed into a lake).
The mother crying, in fact, doesn't matter at all.

When rage fills the killer's cranial lobe,
no guilt spills from the wound's endless helix.

According to his cousin, the murderer, as a boy, stabbed his birthday
pup with a stick *for following him around.*

Re-enactment: Trapped in a prison van, the pup stabber peels
tape from his shoe bottom to reveal a key.

He unshackles himself, climbs out of the van's roof,
slips off the back and stumbles to freedom.

Several versions of Silvestre fill the screen: Reinaldo with a beard,
Reinaldo with glasses sans beard, Reinaldo long haired,

Reinaldo with a shaved head. At the end of the show,
the gynecomast shakes John Walsh's small hands.

John remembers his son, Adam, bricked, guttered
under some bridge. He swears to the lens:

we will find them.

THE DEAD

. . . and those useless, homeless, I mean, they didn't have the decency
to say they'd gone . . .
　　　　　　　—Anonymous Radio Caller

Before they charged in, did the firemen imagine rags,
hundreds and dense about the box boards,

a mountain of bodies in the ice-house, insulated
mass of stains, a moan. Would they hose down

and snatch out who they could?
Beyond the piss stinking piles of shit,

imagine the two lovers living there that night, one
hurls a candle. The other kicks over a crate.

Maybe the fight ends before it catches.
Fire begets spoons, bricks, a back draft.

Into the flames, the men go in pairs
after the useless, homeless. Boots burst sternums,

suits broil to bone. One fireman combusts:
two more sear to a beam.

I remember the father on Long Island, trying
to repair his family's cesspool.

He climbed down, and died. One son went in after him,
the brother to save them both — the gases killed them all.

On *Man Chat*, Aussie-Fireman 52 types back: *Sounds ugly.*
I know he's thinking about the ice-house turned super-oven,

the heroes going in, as he would, to give
his life for even those who'd gone.

On the *Boston Globe*, the blown hair and soft jaws
of the president are haloed

by firemen in dress black and brass. *This is our tragedy.*
The sentence scores the photo,

the president's face wet and underturned,
a pink pout, blooming after the escaped.

THE LESSON

. . . I was not born to be forced . . .
—Henry Thoreau

. . . I'm a prisoner with the others . . .
—Tom Sleigh

*

Does it begin by force? To transcend
thatches of skin, one face like another
cliniqued and carbuncled
with slacks,

transfix the great heart:

art is equal to blood is equal to the savage that you aren't.
In the abyss, you sing *I am clear. I am all parts of the whole.*
I am the whole. Where
do you fit?

Do you never want to break out
dancing in the middle of a crowded room:
or is the organic you a fine wisp, a god
of good hair, a saint shot out to space?

*

When the wind pushes against my house
and it feels like it might fall into itself,
I am a cardhouse.

On *Real T.V.*, in a suburb, caught on video
white teens sledgehammer
the toilets and tubs of a friend.

In the trail of boric acid I lay out for the roaches,
do the vermin know bleach, flour — they are about to be killed?

How do you know by force
or equation a chasm, a magnet

a soul

or by what word is beauty —
begin with being a bore
or being bored through in a market,
the surprise, each time, in being called, *sir*.

*

Side B: aesthetic theory — Your skin is pink,
then opaque, caramelized then burned
if you are one of the drumsticks
stuffed in a bowl, as in holocaust.

NY Times, East Timor. A blown-apart leg unskinned,
a shoe's sole ripped back to bone, synonym
for torso in a soccer shirt.

This is ours. We are pickled, you
and me with this strange leg.
Should I turn the chicken over?

See your life as screenic,
think collage,
ethnograph — He is your brown body.

Buy Chanel, Egoiste,
a black border. When I turn the page: *crack*
the bone and scrape out the marrow
for marinade.

*

You do not fall from the sky
en route to Paris, but die in the flash flood
mud with the others.

Salamanders roil. The Silverbacks
peep out of their jungle.

Finally, the deserved. Your body laid without
a listerined and living mouth.

*

How to love the wisp of your face,
the not watching out
the knowing in being clear
and white:

Not on the margin
nor pushed out
on smack, on safari, I am
an ellipsis.

I do not come in peace

for the flesh that stinks
of the heart and bone you've devoured.

Transcend: I am a face
ready to cut into you
stalagmites by fist.

Think of razors, think
of obsidian, think

of how and where we begin.

ILLICIT TRAFFIC

Last night, I was surrounded by other black poets.
This statement breaches two important rules about poetry.

One, do not confess you write it.

Such an act is like a razor
found in a field, say *remembered*.

Say you remembered it,
covered with dark brown crud.

Say, when you found it, you thought
it was food, part of a store bought brownie

smeared on rust, in a field, in a park, on a military base,
not in the sand box, below the swing set.

Second, if you are black, you are
a break. Say, a break, one

between a voice that one of us
clefts out, downtown

in a dark theater. One of us sings
the point of possibility,

a voice cracking out of a voice. Not a double
nor two of anything,

which is the real reason in not saying anything
about being this or that. Things get misheard

For instance, after the reading, when I said
this is a great space, and meant us, not it,

she said: *You all could read in a garage and it would be great.*

This dilemma suspends on my wall in a caption:
A cluster of Africans running toward shore yesterday at Tarifia, Spain near Cadiz. . . .

Imagine this, as a third and final supposition, then say you are it, a memory,
Immigrating, the Hard Way, you, a cluster, caught, connected to, it.